E

P9-DSZ-069

LOVE & FAME

Other Books by John Berryman

LOVE & FAME

JOHN BERRYMAN

 NEW YORK

FARRAR, STRAUS AND GIROUX

1970

ry of Congress catalog card number: 74-137749
SBN 374.1.9233.2

FIRST EDITION, 1970

Printed in the United States of America
Published simultaneously in Canada
by Doubleday Canada Ltd., Toronto
DESIGNED BY HERB JOHNSON

Acknowledgments are made to the editors
of *The New Yorker*, in which "Death Ballad" was
first published; and for other
poems to the editors of *American Scholar*, *Atlantic
Monthly*, *Harper's*, *Minneapolis Tribune*, *The Nation*, *New Republic*,
The New York Review, *Saturday Review*, *Shenandoah*, and *The Times
Literary Supplement*

SLEEP! IN YOUR BOAT BROUGHT INTO THE LIVING-ROOM
SUPREME ADMIRER OF THE ANCIENT SEA

YOUR MOCKERY OF THE PRETENTIOUS GREAT
YOUR SELF-REVELATIONS
CONSTITUTE STILL IN ANY SUNSET SKY
A CURSING GLORY

Contents

PART THREE

PART FOUR

Eleven Addresses to the Lord

PART ONE

Her & It

I FELL in love with a girl.
O and a gash.
I'll bet she now has seven lousy children.
(I've three myself, one being off the record.)

I wish she'd read my book & write to me
from O wherever ah how far she is.
After all, I get letters from anybody.
From hers, I'd tear to the 'phone.

It's not now near at all the end of winter.
I have to fly off East to sing a poem.
Admirers, some, will surge up afterward,
I'll keep an eye out for her.

My tough Songs well in Tokyo & Paris
fall under scrutiny. My publishers
very friendly in New York & London
forward me elephant cheques.

Time magazine yesterday slavered Saul's ass,
they pecked at mine last year. We're going strong!
Photographs all over!
She muttered something in my ear I've forgotten as we danced.

Cadenza on Garnette

'If I had said out passions as they were,'
plain-saying Wordsworth confided down deep age,
'the poems could never have been published.'
Ha! a confrère.

She set up a dazing clamour across this blood
in one of Brooks Hall's little visiting rooms.
In blunt view of whoever might pass by
we fondled each other's wonders.

One night she couldn't come down, she had a cold,
so I took away a talkative friend of hers,
to squirrel together inklings as to Garnette,
any, no matter what, she did, said, was.

O it flowed fuller than the girl herself,
I feasted on Louise.
I all but fell in love with her instead,
so rich with news.

Allen long after, being taxed obscenely
in a news-sheet of Spoleto, international town,
complained to me next day: His aim was tell it all.
Poets! . . Lovers & secrets!

How did we break off, now I come to it,
I puzzle. Did she date somebody else
& I warred with that & she snapped 'You don't own me'
or did the flare just little by little fall?

4

so that I cut in & was cut in on,
the travelling spotlights coloured, the orchestra gay,
without emphasis finally,
pressing each other's hand as he took over.

Shirley & Auden

O LITHEST Shirley! & the other worlds

She did not say anything definite; but I twigged
(a word I picked up later in Cambridge, England):
I would not make this one.
No indeed.   Alas!

The most flamboyant fag on campus, P W,
frightened me one Socratic evening
by telling me that *anybody*
targeting all attention to the matter

can MAKE anybody—no bar sex or age
or modesty or toilet-training or marriage status.
He'd been thrown out of seven schools, & knew.
He once gave the homosexual howl

on 52nd Street to Noel Coward
himself, who rose up in the rear
of his open-top chauffeured limousine
& flinging their down-flaunt of the hand howled back.

I sometimes still (rarely) think of P W
& I wonder how his beauteous long blond hair
& heavy bright knit ties & camel's-hair topcoat
are making out in this man's world.

Also of G S, a crony of his,
also queer, who had written half a novel

called 'Fish Out of Water' & was a prominent fellow
among our gang on the Fourth Floor of John Jay
that ran the College.

An old-time novelist myself. At twelve
I wrote a half a science-fiction book
about a trip to Neptune & Ee-loro-a'ala
'published' by Helen Justice in two brown-wrappered volumes,

readership limited ah to the eighth grade
at P.S. 69 in Jackson Heights,
Long Island.   She was pretty *keen* on me
but too tall for my then romantic image.

Besides I was being faithful to Charlotte Coquet
skating up & down in front of her blue house
passionate in the late afternoon barely to be noticed.
O Charlotte Coquet . .

I was political in my first year; very.
With Tom McGovern & Paul MacCutcheon
we founded an Independent Party
to break the syndicate of the fraternities.

I lost the trivial Vice-Presidency
to a combed void from Kent School, Alpha Delt,
by five bare bitter votes.
In two years we had a majority on Student Council.

I recognized Auden at once as a new master,
I was by then a bit completely with it.
My love for that odd man has never altered
thro' some of his facile bodiless later books.

This place is done for, England & so on.
The poet mourns but clamps it to a symptom

fascinating, obscurely foreseeing
the hectic dancer of your delicious end.

O and Shakespeare seized his daring in both hands
to warn the star of the age, acclaiming but adding
something in a Chorus of *Henry V*
on 'favourites,

made proud by Princes, that advance their pride
against that power that bred it.'

Nobody told the Earl, or if one did
it went unheeded,—from a *poet?* words
to menace action? O I don't think so.
I wonder if Shakespeare trotted to the jostle of his death.

When I flew through *The Orators* first
I felt outstretched, like an archaeologist
Carl Blegen himself with his withered arm
I shook in Cincinnati at Nestor's palace:

'Woe*is*me' (the Channing wail
of ladies young at that ladies' school wailing poetry)
that anyone would put great Auden down.
I'd rather prove inadequate myself.

I vow I poured more thought that Fall into Auden
than into Shirley C
the preternatural dancer from Johnson Hall.
O lithest Shirley,—I wouldn't be up to you now.

But darling, sister, do you yourself ever dance any more?
My heart quails as I put this unbearable question,—
into what faraway air?

Freshman Blues

My intense friend was tall & strongly made,
almost too handsome—& he was afraid
his penis was too small.
We mooted it, we did everything but examine it

whether *in se* or by comparison
to the great red joy a pecker ought to be
to pump a woman ragged.   Only kid sisters,
he muttered, want to somersault with me.

Thought much I then on perforated daddy,
daddy boxed in & let down with strong straps,
when I my friends' homes visited, with fathers
universal & intact.

McGovern was critical: I treated my girl *slight*
who was so kind to me I climbed in bed
with her, with our pajamas, an icy morning
when I'd stayed overnight

by her mother's kindness, flustered by my status,
listening then downstairs.
Tom took her over and I ceased to fear
her nervous & carbuncled brother Thornton.

Images of Elspeth

O WHEN I grunted, over lines and her,
my Muse a nymphet & my girl with men
older, of money, continually
lawyers & so, myself a flat-broke Junior.

But the one who made me wild
was who she let take naked photographs
never she showed me but she was proud of.
Unnerving; dire.

My love confused confused with after loves
not ever over time did I outgrow.
Solemn, alone my Muse grew taller.
Rejection slips developed signatures,

many thought Berryman was under weigh,
he wasn't sure himself.
Elspeth became two snapshots in his keeping,
with all her damned clothes on.

She married a Law School dean & flourisheth.
I almost married, with four languages
a ballerina in London, and I should have done.
—Drawing the curtain over fragrant scenes

& interviews malodorous, find me
domestic with my Muse
who had manifested, well, a sense of humour
fatal to bardic pretension.

Dance! from Savannah Garnette with your slur
hypnotic, you'll stay many.
I walked forth to a cold snow to post letters
to a foreign editor & a West Coast critic

wishing I could lay my old hands somewhere on those snapshots.

My Special Fate

I TORE it open, by one end, & found
French prose translations, a French estimate.
I dreamt at times in those days of my *name*
blown by adoring winds all over

and once a postcard came from 'Harold Spitz'
a gentleman in Brooklyn, running 'Huh!
You like that stuff? It stinks.'
One of my first fan-letters.

She was eminent at Barnard.
We sat at the Dean's table
during a prom, and I smiled on the Dean
thinking of her protégée's naked photographs,

and shagging with a rangy gay thin girl
(Miss Vaughan) I tore a section of the draperies down.
I wore white buckskin shoes with tails sometimes
& was widely known on Morningside Heights,

a tireless & inventive dancing man.
I left a dance one night with one Clare Reese,
short & pretty, poor teeth, sensual;
we took the subway north to a waste ground

over the Hudson where we tumbled down
under a trembling moon.
Coarse kids collected to jeer down on us
struggling back up into bra, panties, trousers.

At all times loomed for me my special fate,
Elspeth's haggard unsuccessful lover.

Drunks

ONE night in Albany
on a geology field-trip, in a corridor
upstairs of our hotel
I found McGovern on his hands & knees

heading for his lost room after a bet
which upright I had won.
I read everybody, borrowing their books from Mark,
it took me quite a while to get to Yeats.

I wondered every day about suicide.
Once at South Kent—maybe in the Third Form?—
I lay down on the tracks before a train
& had to be hauled off, the Headmaster was furious.

Once at a New Year's party at Mark Van Doren's
to which I took my Jane & H
cautioning them to behave themselves
the place was crawling with celebrities

poor H got stuck in an upstairs bedroom
with the blonde young new wife of a famous critic
a wheel at one of the book clubs
who turned out to have nothing on under her gown

sprawled out half-drunk across her hostess's bed
moaning 'Put it in! Put it in!'
H was terrified.
I passed out & was put in that same bed.

Down & Back

Iт is supernal what a youth can take
& barely notice or be bothered by
which to him older would work ruin.
Over Atherton I almost lost not only my mind

but my physical well-being!
night on night till 4 till 5 a.m.
intertangled breathless, sweating, on a verge
six or seven nerve-destroying hours

sometimes a foul dawn saw me totter home.
Mental my torment too all that fierce time
she 'loved' me; but she wouldn't quite sleep with me
although each instant brought a burning chance

she suddenly might! O yes: it hung in the air
her living-room was thick with it like smoke
both of us smelt it
blood sludge from a martini

This was during vacation, then my God
she went back to Northampton
& only wrote once or twice a day
in that prize-winning penmanship

I went back to the world sore & chagrined
with a hanging head & no interest
in anything.
It was then I think I flunked my 18th Century

I wrote a strong exam, but since it was Mark
a personal friend, I had to add a note
saying of the 42 books in the bloody course
I'd only read 17.
                    He liked my candour
(he wrote) & had enjoyed the exam
but had no option except to give me F in the course—

costing my scholarship. The Dean was nice
but thought the College & I should part company
at least for a term, to give me 'time to think'
& regroup my forces (if I'd any left).

A *jolt*. And almost worse, I had let Mark down.
I set about to fix the second thing.
I paged the whole century through for five monk's months
keeping an encyclopedic notebook.

I made among other things an abridgement of Locke's *Essay*
down to some hundred pages
preserving all his points & skeleton
but chopping away superfluous exposition.

Mark thought it ought to be published
but we found out there was one in print already.
Anyway he changed my grade retroactively & talked to the Dean.
My scholarship was restored, the Prodigal Son
welcomed with crimson joy.

Two Organs

I REMIND myself at that time of Plato's uterus—
of the seven really good courses I ever took
one was a seminar with Edman met at night
in his apartment, where we read them all

all the Dialogues, in chronological order, through
so that I got *something* out of Columbia—
Plato's uterus, I say,
an animal passionately longing for children

and, if long unsatisfied after puberty,
prone to range angrily, blocking the air passages
& causing distress & disease.
For 'children' read: big fat fresh original & characteristic poems.

My longing yes was a woman's
She can't know can she *what kind* of a baby
she's going with all the will in the world to produce?
I suffered trouble over this,

I didn't want my next poem to be *exactly* like Yeats
or exactly like Auden
since in that case where the hell was *I?*
but what instead *did* I want it to sound like?

I couldn't sleep at night, I attribute my life-long insomnia
to my uterine struggles. 'You must undress'
a young poet writes to me from Oregon
'the great face of the body.'

The Isolation so, young & now I find older,
American, & other.
While the rest of England was strolling thro' the Crystal Palace
Arnold was gnashing his teeth on a mountain in Sicily.

An eccentric friend, a Renaissance scholar, sixty-odd,
unworldly, he writes limericks in Medieval Latin,
stood up in the rowboat fishing to take a leak
& exclaimed as he was about it with excitement

'I wish my penis was big enough for this whole lake!'
My phantasy precisely at twenty:
to satisfy at once all Barnard & Smith
& have enough left over for Miss Gibbs's girls.

Olympus

I‍ɴ my serpentine researches
I came on a book review in *Poetry*
which began, with sublime assurance,
a comprehensive air of majesty,

'The art of poetry
is amply distinguished from the manufacture of verse
by the animating presence in the poetry
of a fresh idiom: language

so twisted & posed in a form
that it not only expresses the matter in hand
but adds to the stock of available reality.'
I was never altogether the same man after *that*.

I found this new Law-giver all unknown
except in the back numbers of a Cambridge quarterly
Hound & Horn, just defunct.
I haunted on Sixth Avenue until

at 15¢ apiece or 25
I had all 28 numbers
& had fired my followers at Philolexian & Boar's Head
with the merits of this prophet.

My girls suffered during this month or so,
so did my seminars & lectures &
my poetry even. To be a *critic*, ah,
how deeper & more scientific.

I wrote & printed an essay on Yeats's plays
re-deploying all of Blackmur's key terms
& even his sentence-structure wherever I could.
When he answered by hand from Boston my nervous invitation

to come & be honoured at our annual Poetry Reading,
it must have been ten minutes before I could open the envelope.
I got *him* to review Tate's book of essays
& *Mark* to review *The Double Agent*. Olympus!

I have travelled in some high company since
but never so dizzily.
I have had some rare girls since but never one so philosophical
as that same Spring (my last Spring there) Jean Bennett.

Nowhere

Traitoring *words,*—tearing my thought across
bearing it to foes.
Two men ahead of me in line in the College Study
about the obscurity of my 'Elegy: Hart Crane'.

More comfortable at the Apollo among blacks
than in Hartley Hall where I hung out.
A one named Brooks Johnson, with it in for Negroes,
I told one noon I'd some coon blood myself

and he spread the word wide while the campus laughed.
Magical mourning blues, at the Apollo & on records.
Victoria, Bessie. Teagarden. Pine-top Smith
the sightless passionate constructor.

Anti-semitism through the purblind Houses.
News weird out of Germany.
Our envy for any visitor to the Soviet Union.
The shaking incredible transcripts of the Trials.

Cagney's inventions in gesture, the soul-kiss
in *42nd Street.* Coop's little-boy-ness.
Chaplin emerging nonchalant from under the tarpaulin.
Five Dietrich films in a day.

Ping-pong at the Little Carnegie,
the cheapest firstrate date in the Depression city.
A picture of me in *The New York Times*
with a jock-strap on, & socks & shoes,

taken during the Freshman-Sophomore Rush:
face half from the camera, hardly any knew me,
praise God in St Bonaventura's Heaven!
Hours of acedia, pencil on the desk

coffee in a cup, ash-tray flowing
the window closed, the universe unforthcoming,
Being ground to a halt.
Inaccessible unthinkable the childlike enthusiasm

of grand Unamuno setting down his profession
in the Visitors' Book on top of a Spanish mountain:
'A humble man, & a tramp'.
Long after, in a train from Avila

I met a cop who called him Don Miguel;
another of my Sophomore heroes.
And David Hume stood high with me that year
& Kleist, for the 'Puppet-theatre'.

Uncertainties, presentiments.
Piranesi's black & lovely labyrinths, come-ons like a whore's.
Gautier rapt before a staircase at the Alcázar
winding up monumental through the ruin to give out on—nothing.

In & Out

NICETIES of symbolism & identification.
The verve I flooded toward in *Don Giovanni*
A shroud, a spade.
Sense of a selfless seeker in this world.

I gave up crew and track after Freshman Spring.
I had my numerals & no more time.
No politics.
I was watching Corbière doomed, John Davidson doomed, their
frantic aplomb.

Shapes of the white ape & his irresistible companions.
My birthday the same as Burroughs',
I had a letter on 'Tarzana' stationery.
He lost his knack later on.

Corridors deep, near water. The surgeon looks over the parapet
& looks straight down in the water. '*Mordserum* sie habe sagen.
Wo ist Doktor Dumartin? Doktor Dumartin
muss Doktor Dumartin *finden!*'

When was I most afraid? Of eerie Wither,
his nonchalance abandoned. Of fragile Elspeth's opinion.
Of a stabbed lady in a drawer at Bellevue
one Saturday afternoon, we peered at Starr Faithful's

stomach in a jar, Exhibit H, avocado-green
Down to the Princeton game with no brakes to speak of
stopping by coasting into cars ahead
I'd never seen such traffic

Princeton had two complete Sophomore backfields
& took us 19–0. But the Brown game,
the last quarter ticking out, 7–0,
a freezing rain on their 2-yard line

& couldn't ball it over
neither Cliff Montgomery nor Al Barabas
my friend with shoulders & bright
who scored the only touchdown at the Rose Bowl.
I still hear from him, wanting me to contribute.

Money? for Columbia?? They use my name
now & then. That's plenty.
I make a high salary & royalties & fees
and brother I need it all.

I sent $100 it's true to Montana
to fund a poetry prize in the name of a girl
I liked in hospital, named Rita Lux,
a suicide, a little masochistic

who was trying to get her priest to leave the Church
& marry her, she pounded a punching bag
with bare fists until her knuckles bled
cursing with every blow 'John Berryman! . . . John
                                  Berryman! . . .'

I learnt in one week more about prose from Pascal
than ever from any Englishman I learnt
though from John Aubrey something, Pascal's polar.
I was tickled by Whitman's also.

And the live magazines were gone,
The Dial, Symposium. Where could one pray to publish?
The Criterion's stories & poems were so weak.
Solely *The Southern Review*, not *Partisan* yet.

After my dismal exile at my school
I made at Columbia a point of being popular,
by mid-November already I knew by name
most of the nearly 500 men in my class,

including commuters, touchingly pleased
to have a soul recognize them.
I liked them, a man of the world, I felt like them,
barring my inordinate desire.

Morose & slovenly, he thought like a tank
the only man in college who understood Hegel
agile enough too for the *Tractatus*
I used to stop by his room, which he never left.

Vistas ahead of what must be endured,
cold girls, fear, thoughtless books . . .

'Dear Mr. Creeley, A reviewer in *The Times*
considering 200 poems of yours
produced over a period of fifteen years
adjudged them 'crushingly dull'; my view too,

though you won't suppose of course I read them all.
Sir, you are trivial.
Pray do not write to me again. Pitch defileth.
Yours faithfully, Henry.'

The Heroes

For all his vehemence & hydraulic opinions
Pound seemed feline, zeroing in on feelings,
hovering up to them, putting his tongue in their ear,
delicately modulating them in & out of each other.

Almost supernatural crafter; maybe unhappy,
disappointed continually,
not fated like his protégé Tom or drunky Jim
or hard-headed Willie for imperial sway.

How I maneuvered in my mind their rôles
of administration for the modern soul
in English, now one, now ahead another,
for this or that special strength, wilful & sovereign.

I had, from my beginning, to adore heroes
& I elected that they witness to,
show forth, transfigure: life-suffering & pure heart
& hardly definable but central weaknesses

for which they were to be enthroned & forgiven by me.
They had to come on like revolutionaries,
enemies throughout to accident & chance,
relentless travellers, long used to failure

in tasks that but for them would sit like hanging judges
on faithless & by no means up to it Man.
Humility & complex pride their badges,
every 'third thought' their grave.

These gathering reflexions, against young women
against seven courses in my final term,
I couldn't sculpt into my helpless verse yet.
I wrote mostly about death.

Crisis

My offended contempt for the mental & stylistic workings of
                                        Ruskin & Carlyle
extended to their advocate,
who also mouthed at me Wordsworth in Hamilton Hall
holding up my appreciation of that great poet

for more than eighteen months.
Later he wrote a book on E. A. Robinson,
a favourite of mine (not interesting metrically
but with the gist of it in him)

which I went into with Schadenfreude
gratified to find it insensitive & unworthy.
O I come here to a tricky old scandalous affair!
He tried to keep me from *graduating.*

I may explain that this man had come to hate me personally.
Not only did I give him hell in class:
I saw my nine friends did. With ironic questions
& all but insolent comment & actual interruptions

we made Professor Neff wish he was elsewhere
rather than in English 163.
I must further explain: I needed a B,
I didn't need an A, as in my other six courses,

but the extra credits accruing from those A's
would fail to accrue if I'd any mark under B.
The bastard knew this,
as indeed my predicament was well known

through both my major Departments. Under the risk I ran
with Neff, I took care to keep an elaborate notebook
on all the readings Romantic & Victorian
to flourish if he got funny. He got very funny,—

leaving instructions not to post his marks
till the last stated day, he sailed for Italy,
and I found myself with a C,
squarely in the middle of Hell.

Luckily the Dean was down there with me,
along with Mark & my advisor Gutmann
& the whole senior staff of the English Department,
because I *had* to graduate:

not only had they put me in Phi Beta Kappa,
they'd given me their major Fellowship
for two years in England
& the disgrace if I couldn't take it up

would be general: only embarrassing
but very that: a plague. But what could they do?
I showed my notebook around & pointed out
the Apollinaire-like implausibility of my C

considering all my A's & my magisterial notebook.
I didn't have to mention personal spite.
They held unhappy meetings for two days.
To change the mark of a colleague in his absence?

Finally, a command decision:
they'd give me a second exam, invented by themselves,
& judge it, & if my paper justified,
they'd elevate the highly irrational mark.

I took it—it was fair, hard—& I killed it.
I never knew what I got, but the course-grade

cranked upward to a B. I graduated.
In my immediate section of the Commencement line

we were mostly Phi Betes, & the normal guys would have
nothing to do with us.

I collected my first installment, more dead than alive
from over-work & poetic theory & practice & Miss Jean B—
a thousand dollars it was—and took off for Canada,
to nurse my dark wounds & prepare my psyche for Cambridge,

a still more foreign scene.

Recovery

I DON'T know what the hell happened all that summer.
I was done in, mentally. I wrote nothing, I read nothing.
I spent a pot of money, not being used to money,
I forget on what, now. I felt dazed.

After some wandering days in Montreal
I went to a little town where Dr Locke
cured any & everything with foot 'adjustments',
on hundreds of patients daily from all over North America

outdoors in a hardwood grove in front of his clinic.
I made vague friends with a couple, the brother in a wheel-chair,
his pleasant sister looking after him.
They were dull & very poor. I gave them tea,

we talked about what young people talk about.
Weeks somehow went by. All this time my art was in escrow,
I vegetated, I didn't even miss Jean,
without interest in what I was, what I might become

never came up, as day by day
I stood in line for the Doctor & gave them tea.
I didn't think much of the nothing I knew of Canada,
half British-oriented, half-French, half-American;

no literature, painting, architecture,
music, philosophy, scholarship . . .
(McLuhan & Frye unthinkable ahead).
I wasn't unhappy, I wasn't anything,
until I pulled myself reluctantly together at last

& bowed goodbye to my lame ducks
& headed for Pier 42—where my nervous system
as I teetered across the gang-plank
sprang back into expectation. I kissed Jean

& Mother & shook hands with old Halliday
and I mounted to the *Britannic*'s topmost deck
O a young American poet, not yet good,
off to the strange Old World to pick their brains
& visit by hook or crook with W. B. Yeats.

PART TWO

Away

Ah! so very slowly
the jammed dock slides away backward,
I'm on my way to Bumpus' & the Cam,
haunts of old masters where I may improve.

Now we're swinging round, tugs hoot,
I don't think I was ever better pleased
with the outspread opening world & even myself
O when *The Nation* took my epitaph.

In fifteen minutes I have made a friend
a *caricaturiste* for *Vendredi*
who has been covering the elections
& a young tall Haitian doctor joins us now

It beats the Staten Island ferry hollow
I used to take to Clinton Dangerfield
to type out from dictation her pulp Westerns
I'm impressed by the *bulk* of the ship

Yeats, Yeats, I'm coming! it's me. Faber & Faber,
you'll have to publish me some day with éclat
I haven't quite got the hang of the stuff yet
but I swamp with possibility

My God, we're in open water
I feel like Jacob with his father's blessing
set forth to con the world too, only *I* plan
to do it with simple work & with my ear

First Night at Sea

I'M at a table with Canadians
He translates Villon. Villon! What Canadian
could English make of those abject bravura laments?
He says he'll give me a copy.

We walk the top deck in dark, Pedro Donga & I,
the Haitian proved a narcissist & we evade him.
He sings me a Basque folk-song, his father was Basque
passing through, his mother a Spanish lady

married, staying there. He ran away
at nine, with gypsies. At the University of Lyon
he assisted with experiments in resuscitation,
he says the Russians are ahead of us in this field.

He sang then for a night-club in Berlin
& got 50 sexual offers a week.
With Memel, the Belgian composer
he went to the Congo to collect tribal tunes.

I listened with three ears.

Now he lives a bachelor in Paris
thirty-three & he has to shave twice a day,
short, muscular.
We trade quotations of Lorca's ballads,

grave news of the Loyalists' fight to hold Madrid.
I have felt happy
before but not in the flying wind like this.
He says come see him at Christmas.

London

I HARDLY slept across the North Atlantic.
We talked. His panoramas,
plus my anticipations, made me new.
He drew large cartoons of me

reclining in my bunk; needing a shave.
(Dean Hawkes had said to me at the end,
about the British differences & my behaviour in Cambridge,
'And, listen, for God's sake, Berryman, sometimes shave.')

Mr Wharton did give me his sad volume
of the medieval genius thief in Canadian.
I told his wife I didn't know how to play bridge,
which (against my principles) was a lie.

Donga debarked at Southampton, tenoring 'Christmas!'
I made up a brief rapprochement with the pouting Haitian
(when *girls* pout, I used to be available)
and then we docked, south of London.

I took with my luggage a cab to the 'Cumberland Hotel, sir'
near Marble Arch, the only hotel I'd heard of
& near Bumpus' in Oxford Street:
we arrived & I looked at the entrance

reminding me of the Hotel Pennsylvania
no place for me, not yet met Bhain, not yet met Saul, O my
                                                      brothers,
& said in American 'Let's move on,
I want a small cheap hotel near here, let's go.'

In half an hour, alive after crossing Oxford Street,
that bloody lefthand traffic,
I was downstairs in Bumpus', O paradiso
where I grabbed the Oxford collection of Keats's letters
& the Sloss & Wallis edition of Blake's *Prophetic Books*.

I went to feel the Elgin marbles, I fed at Simpson's.
Ignoring whores, I walked to a naked night-club
off Piccadilly, leaving early,
& took a 9:06 train up to Cambridge.

The Other Cambridge

Tom Grumbold's bridge has balusters set diagonally
('subtle & very effective')
& a pie-slice of granite is gone from one globe,—God knows
                                                    how,—
upon this exquisite famous by-me-crossed-six-times-daily bridge.

Clare itself in 1359; by Edward I's granddaughter.
It's not a distinguished college: Trinity
or John's or Magdalene, or King's;
but it *is* rather old. It burned & burned.

My Court is brand-new, named for the War dead,
M4 my number.   My rooms look as if they had never been
                                                    inhabited.
My bedder is Mrs Mizzen, pronounced 'zed' as she laughed with
                                                    me.
My gyp: There are no stories about these rooms or this staircase
                                        or this Court.

Anecdotes I collected, inspired by Aubrey;
especially death-words & sayings in crisis.
At the trial of the Earls
ten years of venom flared forth in six words:

when the great Ralegh rose to testify,
Essex called out 'What boots it swear The Fox?'
I liked documents, letters, Herndon's *Lincoln*
for the study of one of the most interesting men since Christ.

Spires, gateways; bells. I like this town:
its bookshops, Heffer's above all and Bowes & Bowes
but Galloway & Porter too, & Deighton Bell
& sparkling Gordon Fraser's in Portugal Place

for days outranked for me the supernatural glass in King's Chapel,
the Entrance Gateway of John's, the Great Court of Trinity.
Slowly, as rapidly my books assembled every afternoon,
I strolled to look & see, & browsed, & began to feel.

Mother of Newton & Wordsworth! Milton & lazy Gray;
imperious Bentley, Porson wittier than Byron,
'Yes, Mr Southey is indeed a wonderful poet.
He will be read when Homer & Virgil are forgotten.'

(Byron always spoiled it by adding 'But not till then.')
Drunks for six centuries while the towers flew
skyward & tranquil punts poled under tranquil bridges:
David's forever new bookstall in Market Hill

where for shillings I bought folios
of Abraham Cowley of O delectable 'The Chronicle':
the 1594 Prayer Book by twelve Cambridge men
& one outlander: Peterhouse' formal garden:

Queens' Wooden Bridge which Newton put together
without a bolt or nail (at last rot began,
they took it down & couldn't put it back,
now it's all bolts & nails, so much for Progress):

Cloisters & the Fellows' Buildings, the Combination Rooms
where wine o'erflows weak-noddled dons: Caius' Gate of
                                                    Honour.
Anthony Eden passed within ten feet of me
in a Chancellorship procession; a film star!

Images, memories, of a lonely & ambitious young alien.
Buildings, buildings & their spaces & decorations,
are death-words & sayings in crisis.
Old masters of old Cambridge, I am listening.

Friendless

FRIENDLESS in Clare, except Brian Boydell
a Dubliner with no hair
an expressive tenor speaking voice
who introduced me to the music of Peter Warlock

who had just knocked himself off, fearing the return
of his other personality, Philip Heseltine.
Brian used to play *The Curlew* with the lights out,
voice of a lost soul moving.

These men don't know our poets.
I'm asked to read; I read Wallace Stevens & Hart Crane
in Sidney Sussex & Cat's.
The worthy young gentlemen are baffled. I explain,

but the idiom is too much for them.
The Dilettante Society here in Clare
asked me to lecture to them on Yeats
& misspelt his name on the invitations.

Black hours over an unclean line.
Fear.   Of failure, or worse, *insignificance*.
Solitudes, sometimes, of an alien country
no book after all will ever read me into.

I gorge on Peek Frean's & brood.
I don't do a damned thing but read & write.
I wish I were back in New York!
I feel old, yet I don't understand.

Monkhood

I DON'T show my work to anybody, I am quite alone.
The only souls I feel toward are Henry Vaughan & Wordsworth.
This guy Dylan Thomas though is hotter than anyone we have
                                                    in America
& hardly at all like Auden.

Pat's reading Conrad through for the second time
'to see if I was right', my new companion,
with 35/– a week from his solicitors.
I buy him *breakfast* at the Dorothy

& we dawdle over it discussing suicide.
He only has two things left (his wife *took* him),
a carmine sports car & a large-paper set of Conrad.
Maybe I better add

an all but preternatural ability at darts
which keeps him in drink.
He is sleeping with both his landlady & his landlady's daughter,
one on the ground floor & one upstairs,

he hates to go on across there back at night.
And I think in my unwilling monkhood *I* have problems!
He's studying with Wittgenstein & borrowing Kafka.
A hulking sly depressed attractive talker.

                    * * * * *

I never went to see Wittgenstein or Broad,
I suffered a little from shyness, which was just arrogance

not even inverted.
I refused to meet Eliot, on two occasions,

I knew I wasn't with it yet
& would not meet my superiors. Screw them.
Along with my hero-worship & wish for comradeship
went my pride, my 'Satanic pride'

as Delmore later, when we were preaching at Harvard
together as kids, he far superior then to me,
put it to my *pleasure* one day
out of his gentle heart & high understanding

of both the strengths & cripplings of men.
Did even Eileen ever understand me sharper?
Many write of me these days & some with insight
but I think of Delmore's remark that afternoon.

Even Cervantes' judgment has not yet wholly overcome me.

Will I ever write properly, with passion & exactness,
of the damned strange demeanours of my flagrant heart?
& be by anyone anywhere undertaken?
One *more* unanswerable question.

Views of Myself

ANOTHER old friend, long afterward,
in the *Advocate* devoted to my jazz
put it differently:
he called it my 'bloody-mindedness'.

I will also roar you as 'twere any sucking dove
these twilight days
but I was hell young.
I did not censor anything I said

& what I said I said with force & wit
which crushed some no doubt decent & by me now would be
                                                    spared
human personalities with shoes on.
I stand ashamed of myself;
yes, but I stand.   Take my vices alike

with some my virtues, if you can find any.
I stick up like Coriolanus with my scars
for mob inspection.
Only, dear, I am not running in any election

I am not my gifted egomaniacal ally N. Mailer

The *sorrows* of the Hero, Alexander's.
The terrors of the Saint,—
most people feel okay! Thoreau was *wrong*,
he judged by himself.

When I was fiddling later with every wife
on the Eastern seaboard
I longed to climb into a pulpit & confess.
Tear me to pieces!

Lincoln once wrote to a friend 'I bite my lip & am quiet.'

Transit

O A LITTLE lonely in Cambridge that first Fall
of fogs & buying books & London on Thursday for plays
& visiting Rylands in his posh rooms at King's
one late afternoon a week.

He was kind to me stranded, & even to an evening party
he invited me, where Keynes & Auden
sat on the floor in the hubbub trading stories
out of their Oxbridge wealth of folklore.

I joined in desperation the Clare ping-pong team
& was assigned to a Sikh in a bright yellow sweater
with a beard so gorgeous I could hardly serve;
his turban too won for him.

I went to the Cosmo, which showed Continental films
& for weeks only Marx Brothers films,
& a short about Oxford was greeted one evening
with loud cunning highly articulate disdain.

Then I got into talk with Gordon Fraser
& he took me home with him out to Mill Lane
to meet his wife Katharine, a witty girl
with strange eyes, from Chicago.

The news from Spain got worse.   The President of my Form
at South Kent turned up at Clare, one of the last let out of Madrid.
He designed the Chapel the School later built
& killed himself, I never heard why
or just how, it was something to do with a bridge.

Thank You, Christine

MET in a tearoom two steps down in Bridge Street;
made friends. Pretty soon I asked her back to my rooms.
As we toppled on my rug
'I'm menstruating, honey: what's the hurry?'

The hurry was a prepotent erection brought overseas
needing to be buried in you
C B, my delicious amateur
mistress of a young interne in London

who comes up to see you once a week.
So there on my floor she did her bloody best.
It was extreme, it was kind.
Once, when low, I made out a list—it came to 79—

she stood third.   Low-statured, dark, sweet-voiced.
I met him.   He didn't mind at all.   Amusing stories.
She painted, & except when painting welcomed me
at all hours until midnight & in every state of acedia or elation.

This might have gone on for months except that something
                                        happened.

Meeting

ONE luncheon party in Andy's rooms in Magdalene
was dominated by a sort of a beauty of a queen
whose charm the company kept enchanted to center on
whose voice & carriage seemed perhaps those of an actress

Indeed I caught on: the most passionate & versatile actress in
Cambridge

famous for Good Deeds in *Everyman*
famous for Cordelia & the Duchess of Malfi
overwhelming in *Heartbreak House*
with a ballet career behind her in Italy

reading Modern Languages now at Newnham
& working up Katharine in *Love's Labours Lost*
for a Garden production at Lord Horder's place
down near Southampton's old estate in the Spring.

I don't think I said a word, although I knew
(as probably no one else there did)
the chance is good he wrote *Love's Labours*
for the Earl & his friends down there in '93.

I couldn't drink my sherry, I couldn't eat.
I looked; I listened.
I don't know how I made it home to Memorial Court.
I never expected to meet her again.

But Cambridge is a small place, & a few days later
she was almost out of Portugal Place wheeling her bike
as I was wheeling mine in. *She greeted me.*
With heartburn I asked her to tea. She smiled, & accepted.

49

Tea

O! I had my gyp *prepare* that tea.
But she wasn't hungry or thirsty, she wanted to talk.
She had not met an American before,
to *talk* with; much less an American *poet*.

I told her honestly I wasn't much of one yet but probably
                                                    would be.
She preferred Racine to Shakespeare; I said I'd fix that
& read her the King's cadenzas in *All's Well*
about that jerk Bertram's father.

We mooted ancestry: she English-Jewish-Belgian;
me mostly English, traces of Irish-Scotch & so on
but long ago, before the Revolution.
Her father is an expert on sleep: praised, pioneered

by Aldous Huxley.   He lives by counselling in London.
By six-fifteen she had promised to stop seeing 'the other man'.
I may have heard better news but I don't know when.
Then—I think—then I stood up, & we kissed.

She skipped dinner at Newnham.

A Letter

I THRONED that woman, up to when she wrote
a letter of fifteen pages—
thrice daily we were seeing each other
in Petty Cury or King's Parade

or her room in Newnham or my rooms in Clare
the fires all well high, or low, the doors locked—
anyway, she handed me this god-forsaken letter
which went, saying, among much else:

Item, we must do it less, it would ruin my health
the which, as well as all my other things,
she for good, she for ever, cherished
& we must both learn to bear it

Item, I was not 'applying' myself
I slept late, I wasted hours with the unworthy
who sought me out, I should be more discreet
of counsel, of autographs, the shadow cast
by my far-envied prize

(But they amazed me, those young Englishmen
so many beyond, in knowledge & debate,
American undergraduates years past theirs)
Item, marriage is outdated & superfluous.

To B—— E——

O UNIMPROVEABLE.
My Tri-Regatta!   My four-minute mile!
My *Antony & Cleopatra* thirsting & burning lust!
My mortal love.

O I was to the least ineffable impression
of a mere ghost of your thought
open, and I'll have it—I can afford it—cast in bronze.
Lesbia lives, past ages; and her admirer.

Too often, as too often you plained to me,
we did it.
'What do you think you are? a sexual athlete?'
You once sighed to me, after a pause: 'O yes!'

Ah, after those years; & later, stark
you lay back on my thick couch in Manhattan
& opened yourself & said 'Kiss me.'
I sucked your hairs.

O my grave love now, probably grey-haired
(horror) & even more (dear love) distinguished,
if you dropped your hand to me
I'd take the next plane to London.

PART THREE

The Search

I WONDERED ever too what my fate would be,
women & after-fame become *quite* unavailable,
or at best unimportant.   For a tooth-extraction
gassed once, by a Russian woman in Detroit,

I dreamed a dream to end dreams, even my dreams:
I had died—no problem: but a mighty hand
was after my works too, feeling here & there,
& finding them, bit by bit.
At last he found the final of all one, & pulled *it* away, & said
                                                    'There!'

I began the historical study of the Gospel
indebted above all to Guignebert
& Goguel & McNeile
& Bultmann even & later Archbishop Carrington.

The Miracles were a stumbling-block;
until I read Karl Heim, trained in natural science;
until I had sufficiently attended to
The Transfiguration & The Ecstasy.

I was weak on the Fourth Gospel.   I still am,
in places; I plan to amend that.
Wellisch on *Isaac & Oedipus*
supplements for me Kierkegaard.

Luther on *Galatians* (his grand joy)
I laid aside until I was older & wiser.

Bishop Andrewes' account of the Resurrection-appearances
in 1609 seemed to me, seems to me, it.

I studied Titian's remarks on The Tribute-Money.
Bishop Westcott's analysis (it took him 25 years)
of the first eighteen verses of *St. John*
struck me as of a cunning like Odysseus'.

And other systems, high & primitive,
ancient & surviving, did I not neglect,
sky-gods & trickster-gods, gods impotent,
the malice & force of the dead.

When at twelve Einstein lost belief in God
he said to himself at once (as he put it later)
'Similarly motivated men, both of the past & of the present,
together with their achieved insights,
waren die unverlierbaren Freunde'—the unloseable friends.

Message

Amplitude,—voltage,—the one friend calls for the one,
the other for the other, in my work;
in verse & prose.   Well, hell.
I am not writing an autobiography-in-verse, my friends.

Impressions, structures, tales, from Columbia in the Thirties
& the Michaelmas term at Cambridge in '36,
followed by some later.   It's not my life.
That's occluded & lost.

That consisted of lectures on St Paul,
scrimmages with women, singular moments
of getting certain things absolutely right.
Laziness, liquor, bad dreams.

That consisted of three wives & many friends,
whims & emergencies, discoveries, losses.
It's been a long trip.   Would I make it again?
But once a Polish belle bared me out & was kind to it.

I don't remember why I sent this message.
Children! children! form the point of all.
Children & high art.
Money in the bank is also something.

We will all die, & the evidence
is: Nothing after that.
Honey, we don't rejoin.
The thing meanwhile, I suppose, is to be courageous & kind.

Relations

I FEEL congruity, feel colleagueship
with few even of my fine contemporaries
Cal, Saul, Elizabeth,
modester Meredith, not yet quite good Deneen Peckinpah

inditing a dirty novel in Montreal.
Bhain Campbell was extracted from me
in dolour, yellow as a second sheet
& I have not since tried to be the same.

Losses! as Randall observed
who walked into a speeding car
under a culvert at night in Carolina
having just called his wife to make plans for the children.

Woe quotidian, woe a crony
glowing on the pillow, talkative.
But dividends too:
Miss Bishop, who wields a mean lyric

since Emily Dickinson only Miss Moore is adroiter,
addressed me in her first letter to me as 'John'
saying 'Surely I may? as if we were friends.
I wrote you a fan-letter twenty years ago.'

Among a-many other   letters never came.

Antitheses

DAWDLING into glory;
or with hammer-strokes.
Our friends have taken both ways.
I'll put the first way first.

Mooning, wishers,
unable to make up our mind like a practical man
about *anything*.
The first time I saw Wystan Auden his socks didn't match.

Only—the other path—we are *hard-headed*.
Victor Hugo (not one of my favourite authors,
except for, in *Les Orientales*, 'Les Djinns')
wrote down each night to the end of his passionate life
the exact sums he paid Joséphine & Héloise.

So: we moon; we tough.
Nobody can make head or tail of us.
Plato threw us *out*.
Freud threw out a hint about Leonardo . .

International art: . . . I feel *friendly* to the idea
but skeptical.
I live at 33 Arthur Ave. S. E.
& mostly write from here.

My rocking-chair is dark blue, it's in one corner
& swivels, as my thought drifts.
My wife's more expensive patchquilt rocker
is five feet away & does not swivel.

The Soviet Union

THERE was that business in Siberia, in '19.
That was disgusting.
My God if John Adams had foreseen that
he would have renounced his immortality.

It was despicable.   My friends, forgive us.
It was done by our fearful invasive fathers.
I have a Russian image: in the Crimea, a train is stalled:
She's in labour, lanterns are swinging,

they couldn't help her.   She hemorrhaged, among the peasants,
grimaced; & went away.
And Nikolay struck down in the advance
seeing the others going on

thought Am I wounded?   Maybe I will die!
ME, Nikolay Rostov, whom everybody *loved* so?

You murdered Babel,
we murdered Martin Luther King; redskins, blacks.
You have given a bitter time to Jews.
Maybe one of our Negroes was a Babel.

Trotsky struggled: over the railway system
and which troops were when to be where.
When he addressed the Petrograd Soviet
their vascular systems ran vodka.

Lenin wrote: Stalin is a boor;
& should not continue as Secretary.

Lenin, that great man, dying off there,
with only her (that great woman) to talk to.

Stalin was mad at midnight: & criminal.   But that Georgian had
high even heroic qualities,
He stayed you through the horrible advance
of the German divisions.   He had faith.
Smolensk; & then in the South.

An Odessa Jew, a bespectacled intellectual small man,
who rode with the revolutionary Cossacks,
was murdered in one of your prisons or your camps.
Man is vicious.   We forgive you.

The Minnesota 8 and the Letter-Writers

Here's one who wants them *hanged*. A poor sick mind,
signing itself & saying where it's from:
St Louis Park. Out of the woodwork vermin come.

To crises rise our worst, and (some) our best
to dare illegal deeds in an unpopular cause
defying prison because they feel they ought, because

the sanity & honour seem endangered,
or seem convulsed, of their own country, and
a flaccid people can't be got to understand

its state without some violence undertaken,
by somebody without a thing to gain,
to shock it into resisting,—one program pain

of treatment back to the health of the body politic:
to stop napalming pint-sized yellow men
& their slant-eyed children, and ground arms & come home again.

O the Signers broke the law, and deserved hanging,
by the weird light of the sage of St Louis Park,
who probably admires *them*. *These* bear their rare mark.

Regents' Professor Berryman's Crack on Race

Lᴇᴛ's confront, Blackie!   I concur with you,
we cannot live together in one place
without—so Jefferson predicted—*war*,
    and neither of us wants war

or do you?   Some to beat off Whitey's balls
are passionate—we won't put up with that,
even our nigger-lovers, or, maybe they will!
    no longer, according to you, after all having any.

There's a hell of a concern on both sides with balls.
The complex & awful thought of my colleague Ralph Ellison
most of you don't know a goddamned thing about,
    any more than most of us do.

No amends, clearly, but there is forgiveness;
which only the very good will beg and saints
out of their love for someone Other grant
    or merely out of their dignity & counter-humility.

At least your camp & ours might camp together,
your wise ones brood by ours, and your fanatics
armed by the Pentagon with our fanatics
    have it out & good riddance.

You don't buy that idea?   No more, exactly, do I;
I chuckle it on in passing, as: not practical
but bloody, sacrificial, since the Blues
    the most promising mutual drama.

Have a Genuine American Horror-&-Mist on the Rocks

(14,500 six-ton concrete-&-steel vaults of nerve-gas rockets,
lethal)

THE terrible trains crawl seaward thro' the South,
where TV teams quiz small-town citizens:
'Waal . . if the Army says it's safe, it's okay with me.
Ah've got a boy in Veetnam.'

All this mad stuff has been there fifteen years!
leaking its coffins. Had the Chinese come
down in Korea, who knows? then or now knows?
Nobody *knows anything*

but somewhere up in the murky constellation
of Government & the scientists & the military
responsible to no-one someone knows
that he too doesn't know anything

and can't say what would then have happened or will 'now'
happen

on the Atlantic bottom in the long dark
of decades of ecology to come
while the 20th Century flies insanely on.

To a Woman

The problem is urgent, yes, for this hot light
we so love may not last.
Man seems to be darkening himself;
you must still for some & the other depend on him,
but perhaps essentially now it is your turn.

Your three sons, your political career,
your husband's legal work & fervency in bed,
your story-writing, your great bodily freshness
at thirty-one now, yes, for the problem is urgent
as a spasm of diarrhoea.

You must perhaps both pray for & abandon
your peculiar strength of patience,
daring daily more or all.
Oddly crowned with a solitary ailanthus,
the tortured red hills to this hot light swell with pride.

A Huddle of Need

I WONDERED about their things.   Were they large or small?
Sensitive, or not?
Reddish, or otherwise?
Then I undertook research in this subject.

No woman I ever came on was satisfied with them.
Too large! Too small!
'They're not interesting.'
But O my thin small darling, they are yours.

Woe the Toltecs, & everything is forgotten
almost but stately terraces.   I think so, and
the terrors of the knife.
Maybe the sex of the knife made a difference.

I will say: I have been wrong.
And God settled the Jews in Odessa
when he might have put them in Jerusalem
I go now this far, in the Book of Babel.

I seldom now go out.   She's out of town.
After all has been said, and all *has* been said,
Man is a huddle of need.
Having explained so much, I close my mouth.

Damned

DAMNED. Lost & *damned*. And I find I'm pregnant.
It must have been in a shuffle of disrobing
or shortly after.
I confess: I don't know what to do.

She wept steadily all thro' the performance.
As soon as I tucked it in she burst into tears.
She had a small mustache but was otherwise gifted,
riding, & crying her heart out.

(She had been married two years) I was amazed.
(Her first adultery) I was scared & guilty.
I said 'What are you crying for, darling? *Don't.*'
She stuttered something & wept on.

She came again & again, twice ejecting me
over her heaving. I turned my head aside
to avoid her goddamned tears,
getting in my beard.

I am busy tired mad lonely & old.
O this has been a long long night of wrest.

I saw her once again: on a busy sidewalk
outside a grocery store
& she was big & I did *not* say 'Is it mine?'
I congratulated her.

Brighter it waxeth; it's almost seven.

Of Suicide

REFLEXIONS on suicide, & on my father, possess me.
I drink too much.   My wife threatens separation.
She won't 'nurse' me.   She feels 'inadequate'.
We don't mix together.

It's an hour later in the East.
I could call up Mother in Washington, D.C.
But could she help me?
And all this postal adulation & reproach?

A basis rock-like of love & friendship
for all this world-wide madness seems to be needed.
Epictetus is in some ways my favourite philosopher.
Happy men have died earlier.

I still plan to go to Mexico this summer.
The Olmec images!   Chichén Itzá!
D. H. Lawrence has a wild dream of it.
Malcolm Lowry's book when it came out I taught to my precept
                                                    at Princeton.

I don't entirely resign.   I may teach the Third Gospel
this afternoon.   I haven't made up my mind.
It seems to me sometimes that others have easier jobs
& do them worse.

Well, we must labour & dream.   Gogol was impotent,
somebody in Pittsburgh told me.

I said: At what age?   They couldn't answer.
That is a damned serious matter.

Rembrandt was sober.   There we differ.   Sober.
Terrors came on him.   To us too they come.
Of suicide I continually think.
Apparently he didn't.   I'll teach Luke.

Dante's Tomb

A TIRED banana & an empty mind
at 7 a.m.   My world offends my eyes
bleary as an envelope cried-over
after the letter's lost.

In spite of it all, both it & me,
I'll chip away at the mystery.
There's a Toltec warrior in Minneapolis
with narrow eyes, reclining.

The head raised & facing you;
larger than life-size, in tan granite.
The cult perished.
The empty city welcomed the monkeys.

We don't *know*.   Hundreds & hundreds of little poems
rolled up & tied with ribbons
over the virgin years, 'unwanted love'.
And Miss Bishop's friend has died,

and I will die and one day in Ravenna
I visited his tomb.   A domed affair,
forbidding & tight shut.
'Dantis Poetae Sepulchrum.'

She said to me, half-strangled, 'Do that again.
And then do the other thing.'
Sunlight flooded the old room
& I was both sleepy & hungry.

Despair

Iᴛ seems to be ᴅᴀʀᴋ all the time.
I have difficulty walking.
I can remember what to say to my seminar
but I don't know that I want to.

I said in a Song once: I am unusually tired.
I repeat that & increase it.
I'm vomiting.
I broke down today in the slow movement of K.365.

I certainly don't think I'll last much longer.
I wrote: 'There may be horribles.'
I increase that.
(I think she took her little breasts away.)

I am in love with my excellent baby.
Crackles! in darkness ʜᴏᴘᴇ; & disappears.
Lost arts.
Vanishings.

Walt!   We're downstairs,
even you don't comfort me
but I join your risk my dear friend & go with you.
There are no matches

Utter, His Father, one word

The Hell Poem

Hospital racket, nurses' iron smiles.
Jill & Eddie Jane are the souls.
I like nearly all the rest of them too
except when they feed me paraldehyde.

Tyson has been here three heavy months;
heroin.   We have the same doctor: She's improving,
let out on pass tonight for her first time.
A madonna's oval face with wide dark eyes.

Everybody is jolly, patients, nurses,
orderlies, some psychiatrists.   Anguishes;
gnawings.   Protractions of return
to the now desired but frightful outer world.

Young Tyson hasn't eaten since she came back.
She went to a wedding, her mother harangued her
it was all much too much for her
she sipped wine with a girl-friend, she fled here.

Many file down for shock & can't say after
whether they ate breakfast. Dazed till four.
One word is: the memory will come back.
Ah, weeks or months.   Maybe.

Behind the locked door, called 'back there',
the worse victims.
Apathy or ungovernable fear
cause them not to watch through the window starlight.

73

They can't have matches, or telephone.   They slob food.
Tantrums, & the suicidal, are put back there.
Sometimes one is promoted here.   We are ecstatic.
Sometimes one has to go back.

It's all girls this time.   The elderly, the men,
of my former stays have given way to girls,
fourteen to forty, raucous, racing the halls,
cursing their paramours & angry husbands.

Nights of witches: I dreamt a headless child.
Sobbings, a scream, a slam.
Will day glow again to these tossers, and to me?
I am staying days.

Death Ballad

('I don't care')

Tyson & Jo, Tyson & Jo
became convinced it was no go
& decided to end it all
at nineteen,—on the psychiatric ward.

Trouble is, Tyson was on the locked ward,
Jo for some reason on the open
and they were forbidden to communicate
either their love or their hate.

Heroin & the cops were Tyson's bit
I don't know just what Jo's was, ah but it
was more self-destructive still.
She tried to tear a window & screen out.

United in their feel of worthlessness
& rage, they stood like sisters in their way
blocking their path.   They made a list
of the lies of Society & glared: 'We don't exist.'

The charismatic quality of these charming & sensitive girls
smiled thro' their vices; all were fond of them
& wished them well.
They sneered: 'We prefer Hell.'

What will their fates be? Put their heads together,
in their present mental weather,
no power can prevent their dying.   That is so.
Only, Jo & Tyson, Tyson & Jo,

take up, outside your blocked selves, some small thing
that is moving
& wants to keep on moving
& needs therefore, Tyson, Jo, your loving.

'I Know'

Revelations every two hours on the Lounge.
So Hilary 17 tried suicide.
She goes barefooted & quizzically laughs.
There seems nothing wrong with her.

Her father found her.   At the hospital they shot her several
                                                    times in the hip.
A bottle and a half of sleeping pills.
She came out of it, not even nauseated;
'I have a tough stomach.'

O Tyson: 'I don't *think* any more.   I *know*.'

And Bertrand Russell's little improbable son
said to his teacher, a friend of ours at Princeton,
when they came to 'two plus two equals four'
piped up 'My *father* isn't sure of that.'

Ah at all levels.   Many of the sane
walking the streets like trees
are weirder than my mournful fellow-patients;
they hide it better.

Laana's husband's lawyer served papers this afternoon.
That excellent & even noble woman cried as we sat on the
                                                    Lounge.
The architecture of the locked ward leaves much to be desired.
A private conversation with mad Tyson
infeasible.   Jeff, 6′ 4″, 18, paws my right arm, & cries.

77

Purgatory

THE days are over, I leave after breakfast
with fifteen hundred things to do at home;
I made just now my new priority list.
Who will I miss?

Paul Bauer at 3 a.m. with his fine-going story
I cover over with him word by word
controlling the reader to do half the work
but forcing each sentence-series interesting?

Marcia, 15, tall, with her sweet shy grin
& low-voiced question
'Do you think I belong here like the others?'
against the piano, the pool- & ping-pong tables?

Greg who wandered into my room at midnight
& rehearsed to me (exhausted)
with finite iteration & wild pauses
his life-story?   He retired two years ago
& hasn't had a good day or a good night since.

Some of the rest?   Yes, yes!   except for the black lady
who told us on Wednesday morning in the Group
she was going to suicide between 62 and 67.
Arrogant, touchy, vain, self-pitying, & insolent:

I haven't been spoken to so for thirteen years.
In print of course they insult you, & who cares?   But in person?
O no I won't miss *her*.   But Mrs Massey,
long widowed, long retired, frail, toothpick-thin,

grew bored, & manages, with a withered smile
for each sole patient, our downstairs dining-room
at the evening eat. We have been friends for years
on my returnings, her survival. Late in a dinner
she stops by whatever table I am at

& bends over: 'Mr Berryman, was everything all right?'
Tonight though she touched my elbow afterward
as I was bearing my cleared tray to the rack:
'It gives me honour to serve a man like you,

would you sometime write me out a verse or two & sign it?'
O my brave dear lady, yes I will.
This is it.
I certainly will miss at 6:25 p.m. you.

And if *you* can carry on so, so maybe can I.

Heaven

F<small>REE</small>! while in the cathedral at Seville
a Cardinal is singing.   I bowed my face
& licked the monument.   Aged women
waited behind me.   Free! to lick & believe,

Free free! on an Easter afternoon
I almost said I loved her, we held hands
in the cemetery.   Choirs came down on us,
St Anselm bothered his ecstatic repose to chide.

Ambrose interpreted: I was in love with her,
she was half with me.   Among the tombs.
She was killed in a car accident soon after she married,
a lissom light-haired alluring phantastic young lady.

Fly by, spirits of Night, her cenotaph
& forgive my survival with one shoe.
She forgave me that golden day my lust for her
but what might persuade me to forgive her loss?

Allow her exalted kind forbidding voice
a place in the *Lachrymosa.*
Let her sing on.
O lucky spirits to sing on with her.

Then *a capella:* mourning, barely heard,
across the Venetian waters: louder, dear,
I have a 15% hearing loss from a childhood illness,
louder, my darling, over at San Giorgio.

The Home Ballad

WE must work & play and John Jacob Niles
will sing our souls to rest
(in his earlier-78 recordings).
Tomorrow we'll do our best, our best,
tomorrow we'll do our best.

The income tax is done, is done,
and three full weeks before
& it's going to be O very bad
but the medical expenses are more, are more,
the medical & support are more.

I left the place with one cracked toe,
at noon I packed in haste
out of that hospital O to go
they wanted me to stay, to stay
for an X-ray. I said 'Doctors, pray

the thing's not dislocated or broken O
any damned thing beside—
if it is, you're helpless—if it's not, you're a bore'
O I left that ward on my right foot
lurching on my left toe.

It hurt like hell, but never mind—
I hobbled on to free
swinging my typescript book like a bee
with honey back to the comb, the comb,
bringing my lovelies home.

The postal strike will end, will end,
I sent that Nixon a wire
because my ex-wife said I should—
I always do what she says, she says,
because my son sets me on fire.

It's home to my daughter I am come
with verses & stories true,
which I would also share with you,
my dear, my dear,
only you are not my daughter.

Now my book will go to friends—
women & men of wit—
Xerox'd before we publish it, it,
the limited edition & the public it,
before we publish it.

It's *Love & Fame* called, honey Kate,
you read it from the start
and sometimes I reel when you praise my art
my honey almost hopeless angry art,
which was both our Fate—

PART FOUR

Eleven Addresses to the Lord

MASTER of beauty, craftsman of the snowflake,
inimitable contriver,
endower of Earth so gorgeous & different from the boring Moon,
thank you for such as it is my gift.

I have made up a morning prayer to you
containing with precision everything that most matters.
'According to Thy will' the thing begins.
It took me off & on two days. It does not aim at eloquence.

You have come to my rescue again & again
in my impassable, sometimes despairing years.
You have allowed my brilliant friends to destroy themselves
and I am still here, severely damaged, but functioning.

Unknowable, as I am unknown to my guinea pigs:
how can I 'love' you?
I only as far as gratitude & awe
confidently & absolutely go.

I have no idea whether we live again.
It doesn't seem likely
from either the scientific or the philosophical point of view
but certainly all things are possible to you,

and I believe as fixedly in the Resurrection-appearances to Peter
                                                    & to Paul
as I believe I sit in this blue chair.

Only that may have been a special case
to establish their initiatory faith.

Whatever your end may be, accept my amazement.
May I stand until death forever at attention
for any your least instruction or enlightenment.
I even feel sure you will assist me again, Master of insight &
$\qquad\qquad\qquad\qquad\qquad\qquad\qquad$ beauty.

HOLY, as I suppose I dare to call you
without pretending to know anything about you
but infinite capacity everywhere & always
& in particular certain goodness to me.

Yours is the crumpling, to my sister-in-law terrifying thunder,
yours the candelabra buds sticky in Spring,
Christ's mercy,
the gloomy wisdom of godless Freud:

yours the lost souls in ill-attended wards,
those agonized thro' the world
at this instant of time, all evil men,
Belsen, Omaha Beach,—

incomprehensible to man your ways.
May be the Devil after all exists.
'I don't try to reconcile anything' said the poet at eighty,
'This is a damned strange world.'

Man is ruining the pleasant earth & man.
What at last, my Lord, will you allow?
Postpone till after my children's deaths your doom
if it be thy ineffable, inevitable will.

I say 'Thy kingdom come', it means nothing to me.
Hast Thou prepared astonishments for man?
One sudden Coming? Many so believe.
So not, without knowing anything, do I.

3

Sole watchman of the flying stars, guard me
against my flicker of impulse lust: teach me
to see them as sisters & daughters. Sustain
my grand endeavours: husbandship & crafting.

Forsake me not when my wild hours come;
grant me sleep nightly, grace soften my dreams;
achieve in me patience till the thing be done,
a careful view of my achievement come.

Make me from time to time the gift of the shoulder.
When all hurt nerves whine shut away the whiskey.
Empty my heart toward Thee.
Let me pace without fear the common path of death.

Cross am I sometimes with my little daughter:
fill her eyes with tears. Forgive me, Lord.
Unite my various soul,
sole watchman of the wide & single stars.

4

IF I say Thy name, art Thou there? It may be so.
Thou art not absent-minded, as I am.
I am so much so I had to give up driving.
You attend, I feel, to the matters of man.

Across the ages certain blessings swarm,
horrors accumulate, the best men fail:
Socrates, Lincoln, Christ mysterious.
Who can search Thee out?

except Isaiah & Pascal, who saw.
I dare not ask that vision, though a piece of it
at last in crisis was vouchsafèd me.
I altered then for good, to become yours.

Caretaker! take care, for we run in straits.
Daily, by night, we walk naked to storm,
some threat of wholesale loss, to ruinous fear.
Gift us with long cloaks & adrenalin.

Who haunt the avenues of Angkor Wat
recalling all that prayer, that glory dispersed,
haunt me at the corner of Fifth & Hennepin.
Shield & fresh fountain! Manifester! Even mine.

5

HOLY, & holy. The damned are said to say
'We never thought we would come into this place.'
I'm fairly clear, my Friend, there's no such place
ordained for inappropriate & evil man.

Surely they fall dull, & forget. We too,
the more or less just, I feel fall asleep
dreamless forever while the worlds hurl out.
Rest may be your ultimate gift.

Rest or transfiguration! come & come
whenever Thou wilt. My daughter & my son
fend will without me, when my work is done
in Your opinion.

Strengthen my widow, let her dream on me
thro' tranquil hours less & down to less.
Abrupt elsewhere her heart, I sharply hope.
I leave her in wise Hands.

6

UNDER new management, Your Majesty:
Thine. I have solo'd mine since childhood, since
my father's suicide when I was twelve
blew out my most bright candle faith, and look at me.

I served at Mass six dawns a week from five,
adoring Father Boniface & you,
memorizing the Latin he explained.
Mostly we worked alone. One or two women.

Then my poor father frantic. Confusions & afflictions
followed my days. Wives left me.
Bankrupt I closed my doors. You pierced the roof
twice & again. Finally you opened my eyes.

My double nature fused in that point of time
three weeks ago day before yesterday.
Now, brooding thro' a history of the early Church,
I identify with everybody, even the heresiarchs.

Aᴏꜰᴛᴇʀ a Stoic, a Peripatetic, a Pythagorean,
Justin Martyr studied the words of the Saviour,
finding them short, precise, terrible, & full of refreshment.
I am tickled to learn this.

Let one day desolate Sherry, fair, thin, tall,
at 29 today her life the Sahara Desert,
who has never once enjoyed a significant relation,
so find His lightning words.

A Prayer for the Self

Who am I worthless that You spent such pains
and take may pains again?
I do not understand; but I believe.
Jonquils respond with wit to the teasing breeze.

Induct me down my secrets. Stiffen this heart
to stand their horrifying cries, O cushion
the first the second shocks, will to a halt
in mid-air there demons who would be at me.

May fade before, sweet morning on sweet morning,
I wake my dreams, my fan-mail go astray,
and do me little goods I have not thought of,
ingenious & beneficial Father.

Ease in their passing my beloved friends,
all others too I have cared for in a travelling life,
anyone anywhere indeed. Lift up
sober toward truth a scared self-estimate.

9

SURPRISE me on some ordinary day
with a blessing gratuitous. Even I've done good
beyond their expectations. What count we then
upon Your bounty?

Interminable: an old theologian
asserts that even to say You exist is misleading.
Uh-huh. I buy that Second-century fellow.
I press his withered glorifying hand.

You certainly do not as I exist,
impersonating as well the meteorite
& flaring in your sun your waterfall
or blind in caves pallid fishes.

Bear in mind me, Who have forgotten nothing,
& Who continues. I may not foreknow
& fail much to remember. You sustain
imperial desuetudes, at the kerb a widow.

F<small>EARFUL</small> I peer upon the mountain path
where once Your shadow passed, Limner of the clouds
up their phantastic guesses. I am afraid,
I never until now confessed.

I fell back in love with you, Father, for two reasons:
You were good to me, & a delicious author,
rational & passionate. Come on me again,
as twice you came to Azarias & Misael.

President of the brethren, our mild assemblies
inspire, & bother the priest not to be dull;
keep us week-long in order; love my children,
my mother far & ill, far brother, my spouse.

Oil all my turbulence as at Thy dictation
I sweat out my wayward works.
Father Hopkins said the only true literary critic is Christ.
Let me lie down exhausted, content with that.

GERMANICUS leapt upon the wild lion in Smyrna,
wishing to pass quickly from a lawless life.
The crowd shook the stadium.
The proconsul marvelled.

'Eighty & six years have I been his servant,
and he has done me no harm.
How can I blaspheme my King who saved me?'
Polycarp, John's pupil, facing the fire.

Make too me acceptable at the end of time
in my degree, which then Thou wilt award.
Cancer, senility, mania,
I pray I may be ready with my witness.